30 YEARS
TO REVOLUTION

IVY PAYNE

BALBOA.PRESS
A DIVISION OF HAY HOUSE

Balboa Press books may be ordered through booksellers or by contacting:

Balboa Press
A Division of Hay House
1663 Liberty Drive
Bloomington, IN 47403
www.balboapress.com
844-682-1282

Because of the dynamic nature of the Internet, any web addresses or
links contained in this book may have changed since publication and
may no longer be valid. The views expressed in this work are solely those
of the author and do not necessarily reflect the views of the publisher,
and the publisher hereby disclaims any responsibility for them.

The author of this book does not dispense medical advice or prescribe
the use of any technique as a form of treatment for physical, emotional,
or medical problems without the advice of a physician, either directly
or indirectly. The intent of the author is only to offer information
of a general nature to help you in your quest for emotional and
spiritual well-being. In the event you use any of the information in
this book for yourself, which is your constitutional right, the author
and the publisher assume no responsibility for your actions.

Any people depicted in stock imagery provided by Getty Images are
models, and such images are being used for illustrative purposes only.
Certain stock imagery © Getty Images.

Print information available on the last page.

ISBN: 978-1-9822-6178-8 (sc)
ISBN: 978-1-9822-6179-5 (e)

Balboa Press rev. date: 02/08/2021

INTRODUCTION

THE SIMPLE TRUTH ABOUT MENTAL health is that everyone with a psychological or emotional imbalance can be housed in the category of mental illness. The fact is that we all are imbalanced in some sort of way. Most people with the diagnosis are just more extreme than others. It is okay to not be okay, just as it is okay to recognize that sometimes we need help to process the space of our current status.

THIRTY YEARS TO REVOLUTION

Who was that little girl named Ivy Payne? At the young age of eight or nine, her mom died. She was left all alone. Ivy had siblings but wasn't sure where they all had disappeared to since the funeral. It seemed as if everyone had vanished without a trace. Ivy Payne often asked herself, *Why would a man need to lie with a young girl as if he were lying with his wife? How can he live with himself?* With no clear understanding or grasp on life, Ivy continued to be abused every single day of her life for the next five years.

And she was abused by the only one she thought she could look up to as her protector, provider, and leader. The only one who could partially take her pain away after she had endured the devastating loss of her mother.

After staying with many friends, family members, and strangers, Ivy Payne's life continued to spiral downhill. It seemed as if every stranger in her presence got the opportunity to go hands-on with her, abusing her sexually. The feeling of filthy, nasty, dirty, and bad-smelling strangers too close to Ivy gave her endless nightmares. Whoever knew any of this was going on in Ivy Payne's life?

Ivy continue to search for answers of the missing pieces in her life. Why did her mom have to leave her? Was she even thinking about Ivy Payne's well-being, let alone the emotional roller coaster Ivy was about to ride?

Daisy was a hard-working but strict-to-the-bone kind of woman. She had it all. Daisy seemed to control the minds of others around her, young and old. She lived in a nice home in a good neighborhood, raising her children with her husband of twenty years. Being in the presence of this well-put-together family still didn't give any comfort to Ivy's broken heart. She could have been surrounded by thousands of gifts and caring people, but nothing would have come close to a mother's love.

Ivy found herself living with Daisy and her family for the next few years or so. Entering middle school felt like torture. All that stayed on Ivy Payne's mind was one thing: when would she see her mother again?

Ivy Payne had to digest the harsh words that she overheard pertaining to her situation. It was like she was picked and plucked around like a fleeing bug, in and out of strangers' homes, taking the subway back and forth to school.

One day while riding the subway, Ivy Payne sat alone wondering where everyone was traveling to. Still, the most important thing on Ivy Payne's mind was *Why did Mom have to leave me so soon? Shouldn't moms wait until children are grow up before they take off and never show up again?* Looking toward the front of the train, Ivy saw a tall, slim woman who reminded her of her mother. Ivy Payne's eyes filled up quickly with tears of joy and fear. Was she finally free from heartache, free from abuse and neglect? Was she in the clear to have what she thought could possibly be a normal childhood? But as the train slowly came to a halt and the doors opened, the slim, brown-skinned woman exited the train.

Things didn't seem to be getting any happier or sadder for Ivy Payne. However, in the midst of her imbalanced life, she had a chance to attend church almost every single day of the week. An older woman named Ms. Magnolia lived down the street from the big house. She would remind anyone of a sweet grandmother. Ms. Magnolia had a few children who stayed with her. Nobody really knew who these children belonged to, but whatever the situation was, Ms. Magnolia took care of them. Ivy Payne had the opportunity to hang out with these other children as long as they all attended church.

Church was really quiet and scary in the beginning for Ivy Payne. She knew what people did in church, but could these church-praying women bring Ivy Payne's mother back? Or just those strong-at-faith kind of people?

Ms. Magnolia had one teenager, a curly-red-head, freckled-face girl. And boy-oh-boy, was she mean as *hell*, in the good ole words of the older folks. But how could Algae be so evil to a girl who had just lost her mother? How? Maybe Algae didn't know Ivy Payne. Just find out about her mother, and you'd probably discover that she and Ivy shared some similar stories. Algae wore her hair up in a red bow and had no interest in sharing anything that she had of her own. Ivy Payne had nothing, and Algae made sure of it. The girls were different ages but Ivy Payne could easily fit into Algae's clothes. Ivy Payne was literally at school with no bra on because she had nothing. The mean kids made fun of her, pointing and teasing her about not having a mother, just mean and rude for no reason. All Ivy Payne could think was, *Why am I so hated by so many?*

With no answers and no mom, Ivy was still a lost child searching for answers. The next few years, Ivy Payne found herself attending school and still hanging out with a few church folks.

One breezy spring came around, only for Ivy Payne to hear more devastating news. There had been a very bad accident. Ms. Magnolia, sweet Magnolia, was in the hospital, and things weren't looking too good. Ivy Payne didn't know much about Ms. Magnolia; all she knew was that a lady down the street had invited her to church with her other children. Maybe she was Ivy Payne's mother in spirit form. Could she have been her second true love that Ivy would soon find out was gone?

Ivy had nothing but sweet butterflies in her stomach every time she was around Ms. Magnolia. Ms. Magnolia fed her; she helped her with her homework; she did Ivy's Payne hair; she even introduced her to the beautiful city of Indigo. She gave Ivy Payne that extra dose of love that she needed. Ivy needed her after her mom's death.

This couldn't possibly happen again. Why would Ms. Magnolia want to leave her children like Ivy Payne's mom had left her? Ivy attended Ms. Magnolia's service to make their final farewells, but it didn't feel real to her. But Ms. Magnolia was indeed gone. She was gone to the same place as Ivy Payne's mom.

That same year, Ivy would end up in another home of a complete stranger. Instantly, as she entered the doorway of the stranger's home, she hated it. Ivy Payne detected the negative energy coming from the eyes of the short adult standing in front of her. Ivy met Arbor. Arbor was a tough one, fancy in style, but tough as nails. By her eyes, she struck Ivy Payne as a cold-spirited woman. Ivy was too young and lost to make sense of any of Arbor's shortcomings, but she knew none of it felt good to her.

Arbor was a slighter rendition of Ms. Magnolia. Both women made sure Ivy had a hot meal and clean clothes. It didn't matter whose clothes Arbor gave Ivy Payne to wear; Ivy wore them each and every time they were given to her. While getting adjusted to Arbor's schedule and expectations, Ivy was growing in age and height but mentally had no idea what each day would bring to her.

One possibly positive thing was going on in her life: as she entered her teenage years, she started her first job. Ivy had no idea what it felt like to get paid, let alone cashing a check and having money of her own. She didn't want money; she wanted her mother, and she wanted her at any cost, no matter what was taking place in her life. No human walking the earth could have changed Ivy Payne's thoughts and feelings. She did her best to learn from her peers about money. She watched and repeated after them to ensure no one would take control of her earnings. It all belonged to Ivy Payne, or so she thought.

Ivy Payne found out she had a love for poetry. Each day in the afternoon, she wrote, writing down all her feelings, emotions, thoughts, and reasons why she cried so deep inside. Ivy created an escape book. She could go hide inside her book, and no one even knew where she was. In Ivy Payne's private thoughts, no one else could hear. There was complete silence, and she had countless talks with her mother. One day as Ivy was returning from work, she began to search all over for her escape book. Ivy Payne knew where she'd left it. But something had happened to it. There was no clear evidence where it was, but Ivy Payne believed Arbor had gotten ahold of it. But why? Why would Arbor want to add hurt to Ivy Payne's heart? Ivy couldn't find it anywhere.

She had so much anger inside of her that she could have screamed. How could anyone watch her hurt? *When is the hurt gonna end?* thought Ivy. For the remainder of her stay with

Arbor, Ivy Payne's thoughts remained. *What a evil fucking person!* That was just about Ivy Payne's entire life in her escape book, and she felt like Arbor knew it. Ivy wrote and wrote for endless hours and days.

On to Ivy Payne's somewhat-of-an-adult life—bartending, kitchen prepping, and government contracting work. She was still full of heartache and pain, but life would for sure move on. Ivy Payne needed some form of love to enter her life. She thought maybe she'd get a great job and meet someone nice who would never hurt her. She was still quite young, tender-hearted, too young and naive to recognize some bright red flag to come. Ivy Payne meet Garland, a tall, brown-skinned, masculine man. Ivy Payne's heart nearly skipped one hundred beats per second. He might just be exactly what she needed in her life. At moments when he would come close to her, she was quite often nervous and scared. Garland's voice was soft but extremely masculine. He knew he had it going on.

Garland and Ivy Payne made occasional moments to spend together. Ivy had no interest in having any kind of relationship with any man if it included sexual intercourse. She was only seeking a hug followed by the words *I love you!*

Almost every day, Garland tried to convince Ivy Payne that he would do anything for her if she only allowed him to have another woman in the relationship. Before Ivy could blink, the duo became a trio. Ivy Payne meet Azalea. She was gorgeous, with long, brown, flowing locks. She soon entered the union between Ivy Payne and Garland.

Azalea had a lot of the skills that Ms. Magnolia had. She loved to cook for everyone; she had a super-high sex drive. *What in the hell have I gotten myself into?* Ivy thought. Garland wanted it all, with nothing to give. Ivy Payne sure enough wasn't on board with any of this negative behavior at first, but soon she'd agreed to it all—all of Garland's selfish ways. It didn't matter if any of the charades affected Ivy Payne negatively. She had no idea how it would make her soul become disconnected and searching all over again for what she didn't even know she was missing.

Ivy Payne watched Garland engage in extreme sexual activities with other women. Whatever she had felt for Garland during the years of their bond immediately went away, quickly shattered into thousands of pieces. What a shame—the man Ivy Payne had thought would add joy and happiness to her heart! There was no chance in hell that Ivy Payne and Garland would share holy matrimony

How could the broken heart of Ivy Payne be mended? She repeatedly asked herself all the time. Her relationship with Garland continued for a few more months until Azalea decided she was getting married. And then she announced she was eight weeks pregnant. But nope, the baby didn't belong to Garland. Ivy Payne knew deep down inside that she couldn't keep ignoring the major issues and problems that existed, sweeping them under the rug and suppressing it all.

Fast forward to a star is born. Ivy Payne was pregnant. Willing but not ready to welcome her baby girl into her imbalanced world. Ivy Payne meet BlueBell. Head full of sandy brown hair. And Yes, you guessed right, the baby was indeed Garland's. Ivy Payne knew that nothing this small and beautiful could be created from nothing less then a he creator of the universe. It was a beautiful present but Ivy Payne had 11 hours of delivering complications, which made her very sad and more and more hatred for the men she knew. She was feeling completely numb to the world. Here she was with no instructional manual on how to care for her baby girl. Trying her hardest to be of the world and go with the first time mothers way. She had no clue as to what she would do from this day forward because mentally Ivy Payne was just a little girl herself. She did her best to stay up with the world of her time. She did most of all the things she was supposed to do at her age. Not even knowing deep down inside she was still that little 2 pony tail wearing girl named Ivy Payne.

Garland was hardly around. He was out day and night Hustling in the streets. He spent only about 10% of his time checking on BlueBell. He had multiple women that he had relations with, he constantly drilled in Ivy Payne's head that multiple wives were better than one. Every time he talked about having another woman he reminded Ivy Payne of her father. A cruel ass man. He would tell her things to make her feel like a village of women could raise multiple children up and support each other while one man ran the household. His whispers to her about accomplishing so much more and so on and so on but after the experience Ivy Payne had with Garland and his multis, she wanted no more of it. The relationship was coming to a dead end. Ivy could feel the cold irony crawling up the back of her spine night after night.

This was exactly the same man that wasn't around when she and their baby girl was robbed at gunpoint headed home. Ivy Payne recalls their very first condo before any youngsters. Ivy Payne was headed home from picking up BlueBell from the sitters. Walking with heavy grocery bags plus BlueBell in her arms she stumbling across a few guys hanging out in the neighborhood. As Ivy Payne stood so nervously at the front of her stoop asking the guys on numerous occasions to allow her to get inside the condo building. The guys aggressively ignore her. One of the men stood up and pointed the gun at BlueBell's head. Ivy Payne shaking and scared, ask the male to please not harm her baby and allow them to get go inside. Repeatedly asking to put it down please and quit pointing it at her baby girl. Within a flash, he turned the gun on Ivy Payne. The weapon went off and there Ivy Payne was, lying in a pool of blood while BlueBell is screaming to the top of her lungs. In the emergency clinic battling for her life. Lying on the surgical table gazing toward the specialist asking him, will she die? You know, was she going to bite the dust? One shot to the face the other to the arm and many long stretches of recuperating.

The relationship proceeded for some numerous years starting with one home then onto the next. Until the day Garland went to jail. Times he was in and out of prison during the relationship was something Ivy Payne didn't even know about. The relationship was indeed suffocating.

He was unable to be seen with just Ivy Payne sparing it. She didn't appreciate minutes with him in light of the fact that most were triggers. Things that aid to her remembering her father.. Ivy Payne communicated to Garland about these things yet he did not even want to think about it. Since he added more torment to her life then satisfaction. Ivy Payne truly despised Garland and all his actions.

Quickly entering Ivy Payne's life was a new male friend that couldn't sit still long enough to enjoy the quiet space that he resided in. Ivy Payne again had no desire to make him her boyfriend. Before getting into anything seriously, Ivy Payne wanted out but carried on as if the raw warnings didn't exist. But the fact of matter is they did.

Ivy Payne meet Poppy. Poppy was no new kids in the block and certainly showed live signs of a hard core around the way guy. But there was something about these kinds of guys that Ivy Payne was attracted to.

During the time Ivy Payne and Garland's relationship was truly sinking. Ivy Payne found slight interest in another man. Computer Love, Ivy Payne called it. She knew that Poppy could give her nothing at all or maybe that wasn't really true. He gave her deep conversation. He actually manipulated Ivy Payne to fully open up without Feeling judged. Ivy Payne was feeling free. She'd visit the computer as many times as she needed to feel closer to him. They'd talk on the phone for hours and hours and hours.

They connected in a way that no other human since since her mothers death. Ivy Payne was Enjoying every bit of it. She felt free even though she didn't have his physical presence there with her. But the day would come for Poppy and Ivy Payne to physically unite. She was really ready for the new chapter in her life. Where at least she thought she was. Soon something very devastating to a Ivy Payne. Something just went left immediately. Not knowing soon enough but he was addicted to street drugs. So why would Ivy Payne stay if she knew that? She thought she could help Poppy. She didn't know how hard these street drugs could affect Poppy and those around him. But Ivy Payne was sure going to try to help him. Ivy Payne was going to allow him to be her very first patient. She was studying clinical counseling and She just knew that she had everything to help this man beat this horrible monster. A few years into the relationship Poppy and Ivy without hesitation moves together. Thus went on for the nest few years Off and on. Poopy couldn't sit still. Sometimes It was like he was in two different place at one time. Poppy didn't have his own transportation but always seemed to find his back-and-forth from our house to his sister's house on the side of town. About fifty-five minutes north east of their home. What would seem like to Ivy Payne that he really didn't have no permanent home address. In an out of the places that he needed to go to get what he needed for him. But for some reason Ivy Payne still loved him, she didn't even know why. On or around the fifth year of the relationship, Ivy Payne and Poppy's rendezvous would be hit with some bittersweet news. Poppy was quite a hard hitter in the streets of hard knock. He was quite know in their local town. A previous charge would now come face-to-face with Poppy's fate. A 20 year sentence for DUI.

Ivy Payne was numb to the conclusion. She felt like her entire world was spinning all over again. Ivy Payne, with the snap of a finger, a woman on her own. Something she was extremely familiar with. She thought to herself, as she walked out of the court room.

Thru year one, they still stayed in touch slightly through letters. It was all still very bittersweet.

Even though he was addicted to the streets and all that it had in it. Ivy Payne realized she had her own addiction and it was Poppy. During those moments in Ivy Payne's life when she thought she had found true happiness, it all turned out to be a volcano. Beyond the outta layers of Poppy, Ivy Payne sort out for one. She wanted the one before the one. Ivy Payne was really working towards rebuilding her trust and hoping she would finally find happiness. But all Ivy Payne really had was another institutionalization situation, kinda like her very own. But still those emotions of Ivy Payne just hated him for breaking her heart, intentional or not, it was broken. She believe in her entire heart that she could still feel the pain. The process for forgiven was far away from a Ivy Payne's heart and mind.

Why did Ivy Payne continue to attract these kind of men? She'd keep asking herself.

Through the next few years Ivy Payne kept herself busy. Working as usual a few jobs. Working in the clinical field. Direct care counselor for children and families. And keep fleshing up her parenting skills, raising BlueBell to her best ability. Ivy Payne really had a true passion for helping others. And although, life doesn't allows direct in the straight path, Ivy Payne still managed to overcome some work discrepancies. Ivy Payne would stand tall and proud to be the voice of some of her abused clients. She took no slack when it came to their family needs. She made this top priority and everyone she serviced knew it about her.

After all said and done, Ivy Payne wanted to be heard: she wanted people hearing the cries and suffering of others. Ivy Payne had dumped some heavy loads and finally loosed to see her dreams and goals, something she had never thought of. Ivy Payne wanted to open the café lounge with a beautiful garden that trails on the outside and people all around sipping infused wine while care freely laughing and spreading love. Ivy Payne could have it all, her dreams were to write an article for the B-Where of Mental Health sublimed company.

But still in the next following years Ivy Payne struggle endlessly finding any happiness in her life. Feeling extremely unhappy and sad about her life. Here Ivy Payne was a woman with

BlueBell by her side. A hella of a poetry writer and fire and desire to conquer the world.

Ivy Payne just wanted to release her true authentic self and free, That wasn't too much to ask for? Not for Ivy Payne. One day while on a evening stroll with BlueBell in the neighborhood. Ivy Payne stumbles across something fine as wine. Ivy Payne meet Calix. It was that sexy haircut of attraction when Ivy Payne met this young man. He was courageous and sexy. He had a gorgeous smile with dimples attached on each cheek. On that long walk home, their first day he asked questions, they chatted about a Ivy Payne's poetry, they chatted about books that he had read. He was indeed different. How? She had no idea just yet, but she could already call it and very willing to find out. Ivy Payne was a active writer, so over the next couple days Ivy Payne would find herself just writing about Calix. writing about their first encounter and her writing went on and on through the days and nights. She wrote so many things about him yet knew very little about him. Six months into this friendship/relationship getting to know him ship, Calix went to prison. Wow right, Yep same thing Ivy thought. What is up with this cycle that keeps repeating itself. Was Ivy Payne in the right neighborhood, Did she need to attend church all over again? Where did she go wrong with her pick of men.

Literally every single man that loved her or rather that she lived in her life that she formed some kind of connection with... PRISON!

Ivy Payne most certainly hated all me walking in he face if the earth at this point. Nothing could save their souls from the heartache that left permanent stains on Ivy Payne's heart.

Ivy Payne wanted a fresh start. She didn't t want to keep repeating the same cycle with men. She also wanted to continue to writing her poetry book and buy a house with a big playground for BlueBell in a few years and continue to be happy every day. Ivy Payne started to fell the overwhelming sensation to life starting to settle in and disturb her sleep. She had no true friends to call in. She considered herself as a loner. She didn't want to be alone but she was okay if she was. Realizing she was dealing with many years of depression and months of suicidal thoughts Laying on her head in the pillow next to BlueBell, Ivy Payne needed a break(a big break). She started feeling sad every day of her life. because she couldn't hear a voice it reason. The voices she was hearing wasn't pleasant, kind or warming. It kinda sounds like one of her dysfunctional relationships in the past.

Day 15 in Posy memorial state hospital. Oh no, Ivy Payne was sinking, but seeing these other people walking around her, made her question how bad she was really sinking or was this all just a really bad dream and she'll wake up any second. What a hell of a change in Ivy Payne's world. Doors opening and closing keys jingling and rattling. Trying to figure out what the hell is going on. Breakfast time consist of patients retrieving the trays from the center of The hall or if you are off restrictions then you can eat your food in the cafeteria was a few of the others.. Sounds like a bit of freedom right? wrong, Ivy Payne still wanted out. Did Ivy Payne hard knock life just come a knocking? If she escaped, would the tramp experience be enough to shake things up for her so she can redirect her seps into another direction. Only Ivy Payne could really break her own cycles. Her very own cycles that she had a major impact in her life. Ivy Payne knew exactly what she needed to do in her life.

Ivy Payne needed to forward focus and follow through. She needed to forget about helping everyone else that only takes advantage of her to benefit themselves. Ivy Payne thought many times if she kept changing her location will she be running away from her own problems, or well she be doing the right thing by cleansing her soul. She was on the right track at one time, doing everything she needed to do for her and BlueBell. In Ivy Payne's private thoughts, please be stand up and be still. This is all a part of the process. She never thought in a 1 million years that she would ever have to experience all or any mental illness to bring her to the next level of her life.

CONCLUSION

On a better note …

ANGER DOESN'T RESIDE IN IVY anymore. She sees life for what it is. She knows her children are well aware of their caretaker and the love she gives. Ivy Payne used to beat herself up, but she can't anymore. There's no space and place to abuse herself when somebody else isn't doing what she thinks that person should be doing.

She's given all she could and had and is grateful to have lived for this opportunity.

She doesn't claim to know it all by far, but she can continue to apply what she does know to her purpose in life.

Season it with Ivy Payne, and you'll taste a whole lot of *love*!

AFTER THE RAIN

TAKE ME IN LIKE A deep breath of fresh air, and then let it out like easy breathing.

Keep smiling.

Stay here to laugh at least two times a day, and make one of those laughs a deep, beyond-your-soul one.

Watch me blossom in many ways!

ABOUT THE AUTHOR

Forced to search for her own identity after years of seduction, abuse, attacks, assaults, violations, and rape. The day would come when she finally heard her own voice and lived to tell every detail through her novels, poetry and private workshops.

Printed in the United States
By Bookmasters